WONDERFUL
WORLD OF
ANIMALS

For a free color catalog describing Gareth Stevens' list of high-quality books and
multimedia programs, call 1-800-542-2595 (USA) or 1-800-461-9120 (Canada).
Gareth Stevens Publishing's Fax: (414) 225-0377.
See our catalog, too, on the World Wide Web: http://gsinc.com

Library of Congress Cataloging-in-Publication Data

MacLeod, Beatrice.
    Birds / text by Beatrice MacLeod ; illustrated by Paola Holguín.
      p. cm. -- (Wonderful world of animals)
    Includes bibliographical references (p.31) and index.
    Summary: Introduces the physical characteristics, behavior, and habitat
of various birds.
    ISBN 0-8368-1954-3 (lib. bdg.)
    1. Birds--Juvenile literature. [1. Birds.] I. Holguín, Paola, ill. II. Title.
III. Series: MacLeod, Beatrice. Wonderful world of animals.
QL676.2.M3325 1997
598--dc21   97-19505

This North American edition first published in 1997 by
Gareth Stevens Publishing
1555 North RiverCenter Drive, Suite 201
Milwaukee, Wisconsin 53212 USA

This U.S. edition © 1997 by Gareth Stevens, Inc. Created and produced with
original © 1996 by McRae Books Srl, Via dei Rustici, 5 - Florence, Italy. Additional
end matter © 1997 by Gareth Stevens, Inc.

Text: Beatrice MacLeod
Design: Marco Nardi
Illustrations: Paola Holguín
U.S. Editor: Patricia Lantier-Sampon
Editorial assistants: Diane Laska, Rita Reitci

Note: Beatrice MacLeod has a Bachelor of Science degree in Biology. She works as
a freelance journalist for Italian nature magazines and also writes children's
nonfiction books on nature.

Printed in the United States of America

1 2 3 4 5 6 7 8 9 01 00 99 98 97

WONDERFUL WORLD OF ANIMALS

BIRDS

Text by Beatrice MacLeod
Illustrated by Paola Holguín

Gareth Stevens Publishing
MILWAUKEE

WHAT IS A BIRD?

Birds come in all colors, shapes, and sizes, from tiny bee hummingbirds no bigger than a man's thumb, to huge ostriches nearly 10 feet (3 meters) tall. However, all birds have four common characteristics: they lay eggs and they have beaks, feathers, and wings (although not all of them can fly).

North African ostrich

Ostriches are the largest birds in the world. They can't fly, but they can run very fast. Ostriches live in the savannas of Africa.

Great blue heron

Herons have large, strong wings. The wings are covered with long contour feathers, which help the birds glide effortlessly through the air.

Feathers

Birds are the only animals that have feathers. A bird's body is almost entirely covered in them. The feathers protect the bird and keep it warm. Baby birds have fluffy down feathers. As they grow, adult contour feathers appear, but they keep some down for warmth.

Where Birds Live

There are about 9,000 different species of birds. They live everywhere, from the poles to the equator. Each species is adapted to its environment. Penguins have thick skins with a layer of fat underneath to keep them warm; eagles and albatrosses have powerful wings to glide and soar.

Eagles live high up in the mountains. They build their nests on mountain crags, clifftops, or in the uppermost branches of tall trees. The bald eagle is the national bird of the United States. It lives along the coasts and around the rivers and lakes of North America.

Bald eagle

Wandering albatross

Albatrosses spend almost all their lives gliding above the southern oceans. They soar on updrafts for hours at a time without flapping their wings. They come ashore only to breed.

Emperor penguin and chick

Penguins live along the cool southern coasts of Africa, Australia, New Zealand, and South America and also in Antarctica. Only Galápagos penguins live in tropical waters.

DIFFERENT HORIZONS

Some birds spend their entire lives in the same habitat, such as a forest or pond. Others migrate, often flying long distances to breed or to avoid harsh winter weather.

The **pintail** lives and nests in Europe, Asia, and North America. It flies thousands of miles (kilometers) to the south in winter, in search of food and warm weather. The species is named after the two long feathers in the male's tail.

Male pintail

Scarlet macaw

The **scarlet macaw** is just one of many brightly colored parrots in the tropical forests of Central and South America. It has a long tail and beautiful plumage.

Parrots
Parrots sometimes live to ripe old ages (up to 80 years). Most can imitate the human voice. The African gray parrot is the noisiest.

BEAKS AND FOOD

Most birds use their beaks to catch and eat food. Because of this, a bird's beak often has a special feature or adaptation that helps it get the food it most likes to eat.

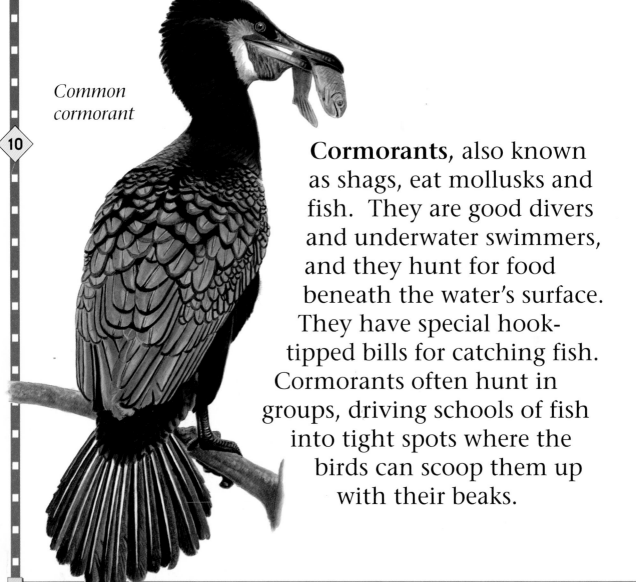

Common cormorant

Cormorants, also known as shags, eat mollusks and fish. They are good divers and underwater swimmers, and they hunt for food beneath the water's surface. They have special hook-tipped bills for catching fish. Cormorants often hunt in groups, driving schools of fish into tight spots where the birds can scoop them up with their beaks.

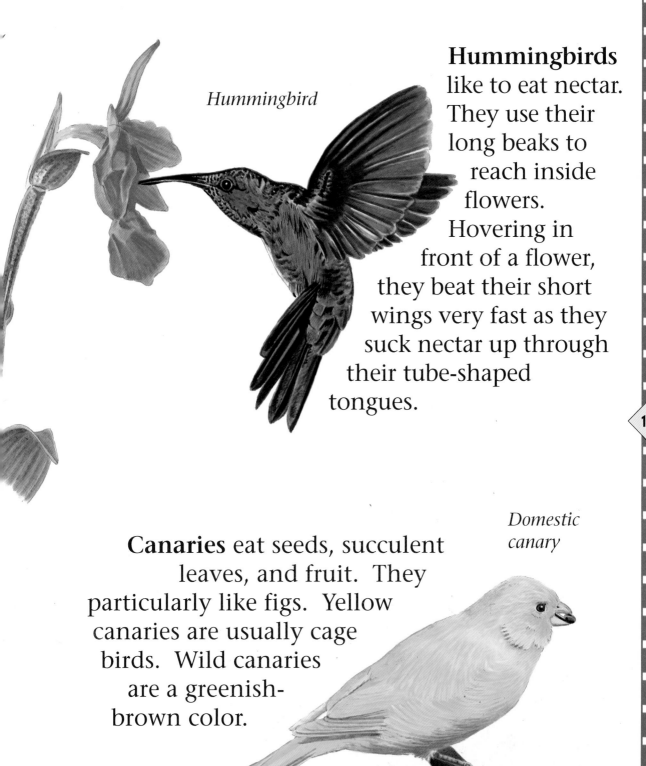

Hummingbird

Hummingbirds like to eat nectar. They use their long beaks to reach inside flowers. Hovering in front of a flower, they beat their short wings very fast as they suck nectar up through their tube-shaped tongues.

Domestic canary

Canaries eat seeds, succulent leaves, and fruit. They particularly like figs. Yellow canaries are usually cage birds. Wild canaries are a greenish-brown color.

HUNTING

Many birds feed on insects and other invertebrates that they catch in flight, pry from bark, pick out of plants, or dig from the ground. Birds of prey have tough, hooked beaks and long, sharp talons for gripping prey.

There are about 100 different species of **starlings**. European starlings were introduced to North America and Australia, where they are now very common. Most starlings have long, pointed beaks that they use to dig up insect larvae.

European starling

Saw-whet owl

Most **owls** hunt at night. They catch a wide variety of prey, including insects, frogs, fish, and small mammals. The owls carry the victims in their bills before swallowing them whole.

Nocturnal birds

Very few birds are active at night. Owls are successful nocturnal hunters because of their large, sensitive eyes and very keen hearing. They can locate and capture a small rodent in total darkness from the noise it makes as it scuttles across the woodland floor.

DOMESTIC BIRDS

Early humans hunted birds and gathered their eggs to eat. The first farmers domesticated a number of birds, including chickens, geese, ducks, and pigeons.

Turkey

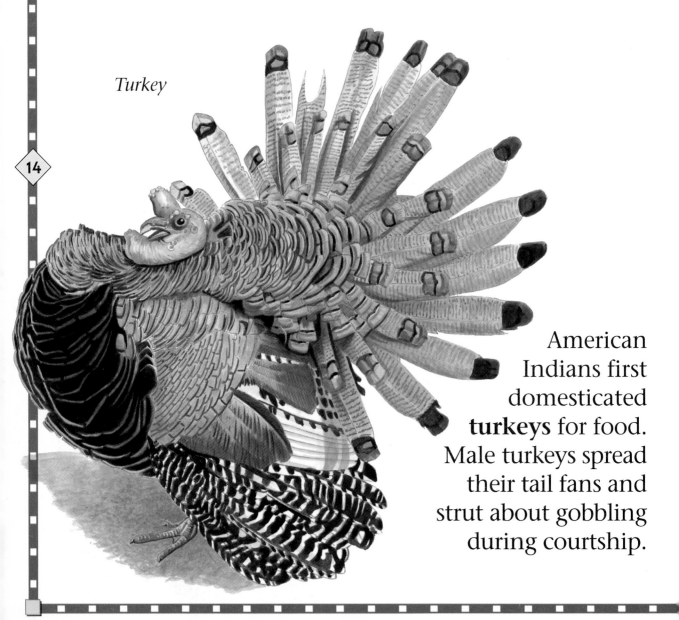

American Indians first domesticated **turkeys** for food. Male turkeys spread their tail fans and strut about gobbling during courtship.

Rooster

Chickens were tamed in Asia over 4,000 years ago. They were used for cockfighting rather than for food. Today, there are over 100 different varieties. They are raised for their eggs and meat.

Domestic goose

Geese are waterfowl. They are part of the same group as ducks and swans. The ancient Egyptians raised geese nearly 4,000 years ago. Geese are a good source of meat, eggs, fat, and feathers.

BLENDING IN

Birds are most at risk when they are resting, sitting in their nests, or newly hatched. Chicks and fledglings often have drab feathers that provide camouflage until they are old enough to fly and defend themselves.

Toco toucan

Blending in doesn't always mean being dull. Tropical rain forests are full of vivid green leaves, bright flowers, and richly colored animals. **Toucans** have huge, colorful beaks that may help keep them safe in their dazzling surroundings.

Some birds change color from season to season. This **ptarmigan** is white in winter, white with a brown neck in spring, speckled brown in summer, and brown and white in autumn. It changes its coat to blend in with the changing landscape so hungry predators won't see it easily.

Arctic ptarmigan

Bright and dull

Many birds have brightly colored feathers. Males are often more colorful than females. Males use their showy plumage to attract a mate and to defend their territory. Females usually sit in the nest; they need to be less visible or they will be caught and eaten.

BIRDS AT WORK

Birds have a lot to do. They must find enough food to eat for themselves and their families, keep clean, build nests, lay eggs, and bring up their young.

Kingfisher

Kingfishers hover above the water until they spot a fish, then they plunge down and scoop it up in their bills. They sometimes have as many as seven chicks, each of which eats about fifteen fish a day.

Common flicker woodpecker

Woodpeckers peck holes in trees where they, and other birds after them, can nest and bring up young. They also peck insects out from under the bark.

Village weaverbird

Male **weaverbirds** build elaborately woven nests using stalks of grass. Females come to inspect, and, if the nest looks good, they accept the male as their mate.

Nests and chicks

Most birds build nests for their eggs. Nests can be woven of twigs, grass, or other plant material and lined with pebbles, mud, feathers, or animal hair. All birds incubate their eggs and feed their young for the first days or weeks of their lives.

Grebes build floating nests. When the young hatch, their parents carry them on their backs.

Great crested grebe

The **cuckoo** lays its egg in the nest of another bird. When the young cuckoo hatches, it tosses the other eggs from the nest so it can have its foster parents' undivided attention.

Cuckoo chick and warbler foster parent

21

Eggs

Birds' eggs vary in shape, color, and size. The smallest egg, laid by a hummingbird, is only about 0.4 inches (1 centimeter) long. On the other hand, an ostrich egg can weigh over 4 pounds (2 kilograms)! Eggshells have tiny holes so the baby bird inside can breathe.

INSTINCT AND LEARNING

Most bird activities are done by instinct. Feeding, preening, and breeding are automatic. But some behavior is learned by copying others. Parrots can repeat human speech, although they don't know what they are saying.

Blue tit

Early in the 20th century, **blue tits** learned to pierce the tops of milk bottles to drink the cream. The skill spread rapidly throughout England as the tits copied each other. This is an amazing example of the way birds can learn.

*Herring gull
and chick*

Young **herring gulls** know that if they tap the red spot on their mother's beak, she will regurgitate food. The chicks are not taught to do this; they know by instinct.

Songs and calls

Nearly all birds can "sing," although they are not all musical. Birds sing and call to guard their territory, attract a mate, or to warn each other of danger. Many birds can recognize their mate or young by their calls. Some birds can sing beautiful tunes.

RESTING

Most birds can't see well at night. At sunset, they go to special roosting places to sleep. Birds also rest during the day. When they are not feeding, they take short naps. Some birds tuck their heads under their wings.

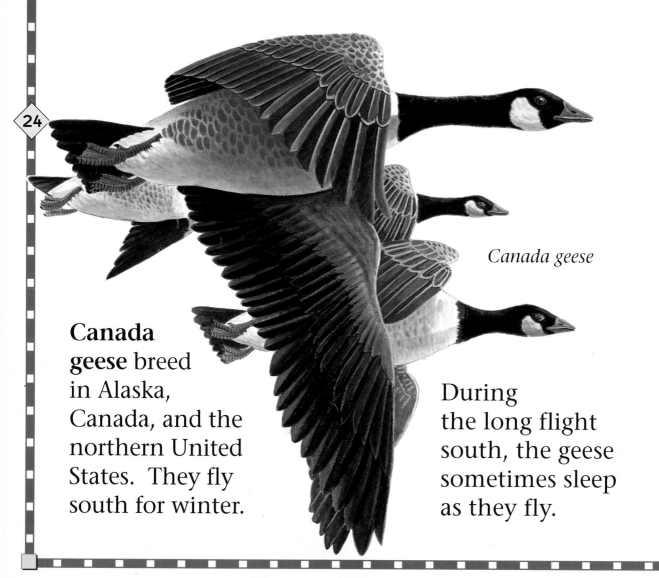

Canada geese

Canada geese breed in Alaska, Canada, and the northern United States. They fly south for winter.

During the long flight south, the geese sometimes sleep as they fly.

Common swallow

In summer, **swallows** build nests of mud and grass. The female swallow lays about four eggs. She sits on them for two weeks. When they hatch, she is rested and ready to take care of the fledglings.

White stork

Like many wading birds, **storks** rest by standing on one foot. They don't like to untuck their legs and, if disturbed, will hop away rather than put the leg down.

UNUSUAL BIRDS

Some birds look unusual because of the shape of their bodies or beaks or the color of their feathers. A closer look, however, will reveal that each of these features has a special purpose and helps the birds survive.

American white pelican

Pelicans have very long beaks, sometimes measuring up to 20 inches (50 cm) in length! They eat only fish, which they scoop up into the expandable pouch below their bill.

The **condor**, the largest bird of prey in the world, lives in Patagonia and in the Andes Mountains. Like many birds of prey, it flies effortlessly, soaring on currents of hot air.

Condor

Puffin

Puffins are seabirds that live in the far north. In spring, their beaks turn many different colors.

GLOSSARY

adapt: to make changes or adjustments in order to survive in a changing environment.

birds of prey: birds, such as hawks, falcons, and owls, that hunt and eat other animals.

breed *(v)*: a male and a female (animals) mating together for the purpose of producing young.

camouflage *(n)*: the shape or color pattern of an animal that helps it blend into its natural surroundings. This provides extra protection against predators.

characteristics: traits or features that help identify one thing from another.

contour feathers: the feathers that cover a bird and give it its shape.

courtship: the act of seeking the affections or approval of another, especially between a male and a female.

domesticated: bred and tamed by humans to get rid of unwanted characteristics and improve behavior.

drab: dull or dark colors.

environment: the surroundings in which plants, animals, and other organisms live.

expandable: able to be stretched into a larger shape.

fledgling: a young bird that is learning to fly.

habitat: the natural home of a plant or animal.

incubate: to keep eggs warm, usually with body heat, so they will hatch.

instinct: a pattern of activity or tendency that is inborn.

invertebrates: animals that do not have a spinal cord or backbone.

larva (*pl.* larvae): the wingless, wormlike form of a newly-hatched insect.

mollusks: invertebrate animals, such as snails and clams, that usually live in water and have hard outer shells.

nocturnal: active at night.

plumage: a bird's feathers.

predators: animals that kill and eat other animals.

preening: smoothing feathers with the bill.

regurgitate: to throw up partly-digested stomach contents; to vomit.

roosting places: places where birds can land and rest, such as branches.

savanna: a flat landscape or plain, usually covered with coarse grasses and scattered trees.

species: animals or plants that are closely related and often similar in behavior and appearance. Members of the same species are capable of breeding together.

succulent: full of juice; moist and tasty.

talons: the claws of a bird of prey.

tropical: belonging to the tropics, or the region centered on the equator and lying between the Tropic of Cancer (23.5 degrees north of the equator) and the Tropic of Capricorn (23.5 degrees south of the equator). This region is typically very hot and humid.

updraft: an upward movement of air.

ACTIVITIES

1. Put up a bird feeder where you can watch it through a window of your house. Fill the feeder with seeds that will attract the birds in your neighborhood. Learn the names of the different birds that come to your feeder. Books from the library will help you. Birds also like to have a water supply in an outdoor container. It's fun to watch birds drinking and taking baths!

2. Visit a pet shop or someone who keeps a pet bird. Find out what kind of care a pet bird needs to have. What is the best food? How do you keep the cage clean? What should a bird owner do if the bird becomes sick? A pet shop can tell you what kinds of birds make good pets.

3. On a visit to a museum, choose one bird habitat to study, such as birds of the rain forest, or shore birds, or woodland song birds. See how many different ways birds can live in the same habitat. Do the birds have the same general coloring, or do they have many different colors? If the exhibit shows nests, see if the eggs of the birds are colored about the same or if they are differently colored.

4. Birds are most active early in the morning and near evening. At those times, look around your neighborhood or a nearby park and see how many kinds of birds you can find. What kinds of birds gather in the same places? Do they eat similar things, such as seeds or insects and worms? How do they act when a predator, such as a crow or a hawk, flies overhead?

Books and Videos

Baby Birds: Growing and Flying. *Secrets of the Animal World* series. Eulalia García (Gareth Stevens)

Backyard Birds. Jonathan Pine (HarperCollins)

Big Birds. (Rainbow Educational Media video)

Bird Watching for Kids. (NorthWord)

Birds. (Agency for Instructional Technology video)

Birds: Masters of Flight. *Secrets of the Animal World* series. Eulalia García (Gareth Stevens)

Birds in the City: A First Film. (Phoenix/BFA Films & Video)

Birds and Their Young. (International Film Bureau)

Crinkleroot's 25 Birds Every Child Should Know. Jim Arnosky (Simon and Schuster Children's)

Desert Birds. Alice Flanagan (Childrens Press)

The Dodo. Tamara Green (Gareth Stevens)

I Can Read About Birds. Ellen Schultz (Troll)

The Moa. Tamara Green (Gareth Stevens)

One Day in the Woods. Jean C. George (HarperCollins)

Web Sites

www.yahooligans.com/Science_and_Oddities/Animals/ Bird

www.olcommerce.com/terra/aviary.html

www.yahoo.com/Science/Zoology/Animals_Insects_and_ Pets/Birds/

INDEX

32